# VETERINARIANS
## HELP ANIMALS

Design and electronic page composition
**Lindaanne Donohoe Design**

Photo research
**Feldman & Associates, Inc.**

● ▲ ● ▼ ● ▲ ● ● ▲ ● ▼ ● ▲ ●

**Picture Acknowledgments**

©**Norvia Behling** — Cover, 3, 4, 5, 6, 7, 9, 10, 11, 12, 13,
14, 15, 16, 17, 18, 19, 20, 21, 22, 23, 24, 27, 28, 29, 30

©**Steve Bentsen** — 8, 26

©**SuperStock International, Inc.** — 25

● ▲ ● ▼ ● ▲ ● ● ▲ ● ▼ ● ▲ ●

**Library of Congress Cataloging-in-Publication Data**

Greene, Carol.

Veterinarians help animals/Carol Greene.
p.    cm.
Summary: Briefly describes the work of veterinarians and includes information
about their education, qualifications, and possible financial earnings.
ISBN 1-56766-310-9 (lib. bdg.)
1. Veterinarians — Juvenile literature.
2. Veterinary medicine — Vocational guidance — Juvenile literature.
[1. Veterinarians.  2. Veterinary medicine.  3. Occupations.]  I. Title.

SF756.G74      1996                                          96-14017
636.089'023—dc20                                        CIP
                                                                    AC

# VETERINARIANS
## HELP ANIMALS

By Carol Greene

**THE CHILD'S WORLD®**

**W**OOF! WOOF! ARF!
SQUAWK! MEE-OOOWWW!
It is seven o'clock in the morning.

The animal hospital is open.
Some sick animals stayed all night.
The veterinarians check them first.

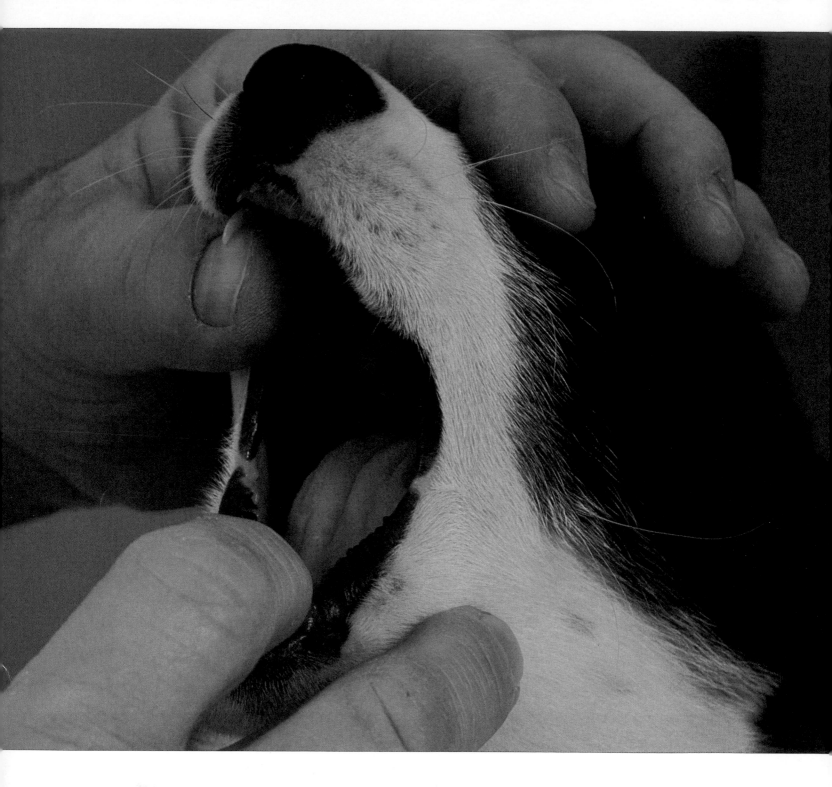

Pat the pup is getting a checkup.
He needs a pill. **GULP!** He swallows it.

Punkin needs an operation.
A vet gives her a shot.  Punkin goes to sleep.

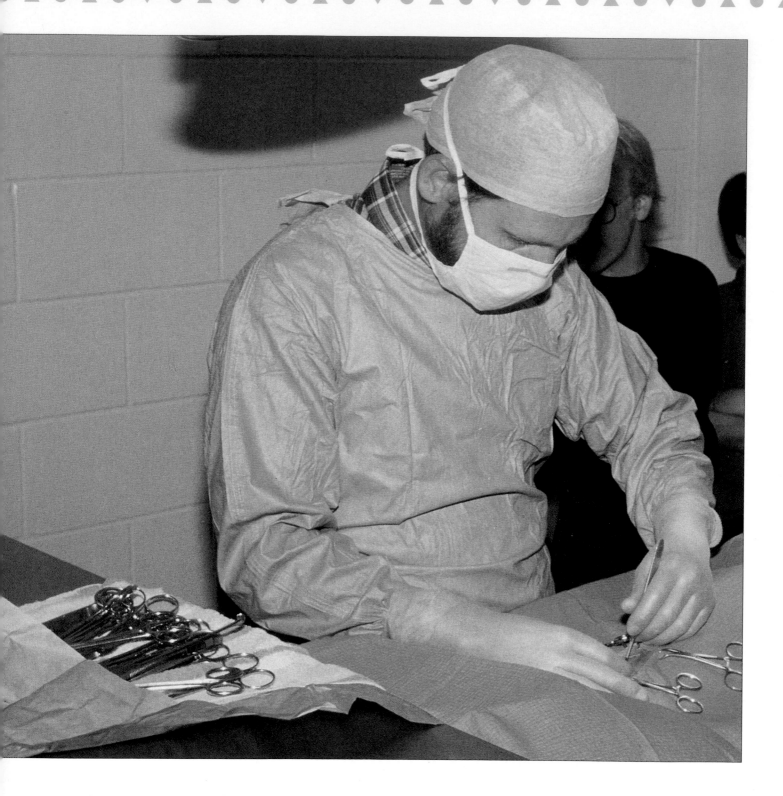

Now the operation won't hurt.
When Punkin wakes up, she will be better.

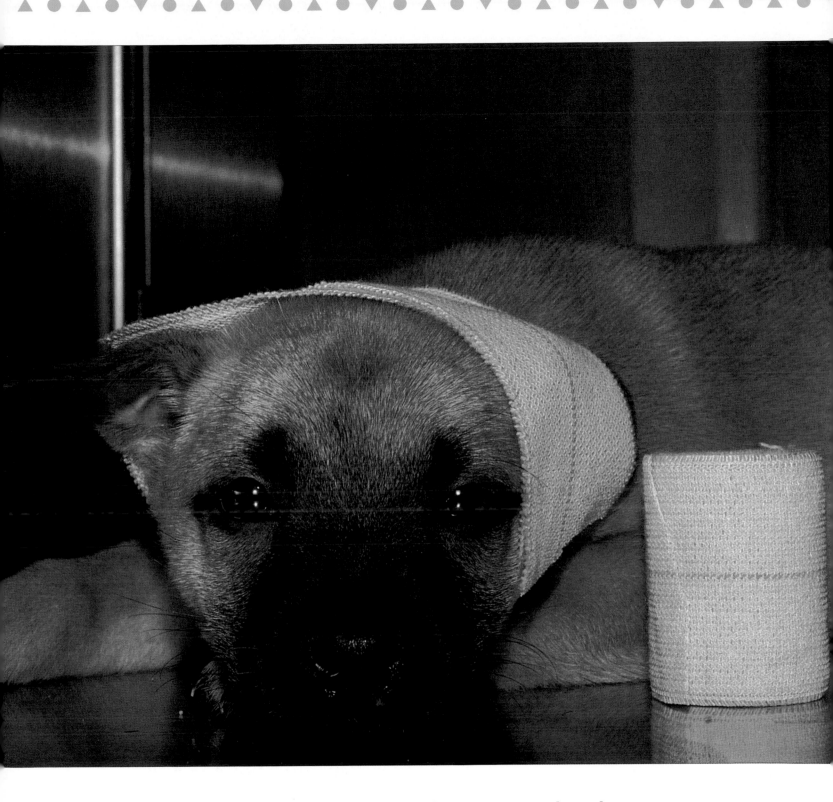

**OWWOOO!** This dog has a toothache.
The vet puts him to sleep too.

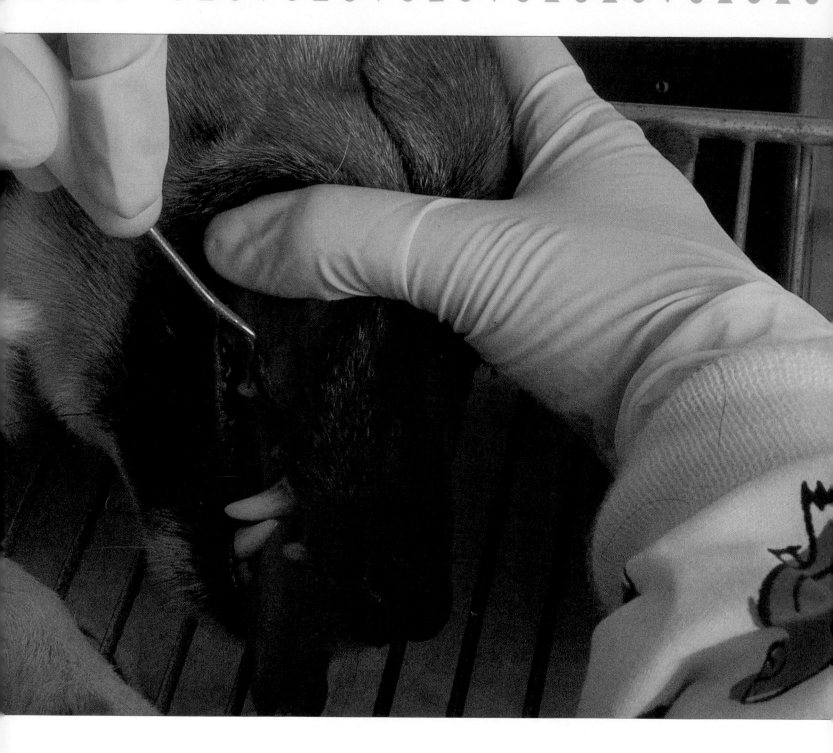

Then she pulls the dog's bad tooth and cleans his other teeth. Veterinarians must be animal dentists too!

**WOOF! ARF! MEEE-OOOW! SQUAWK!**
The animal hospital is full of pets.
A vet checks Puddles.

Puddles is healthy now.
But she needs her puppy shots
so she won't get sick later.

**HISSSS!  HISSSS!**

This cat does not like to visit the vet.

But her owner brings her every year.

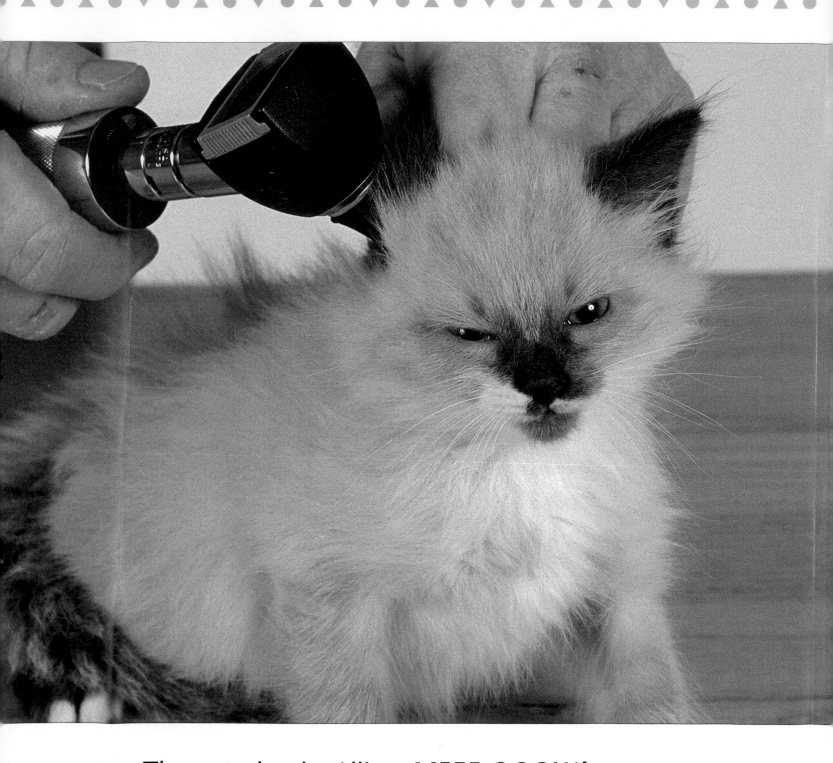

The vet checks Allie. **_MEEE-OOOW!_**
Then she gives Allie a shot to keep her
healthy. **_HISSSS!_**

Quick!  Get a vet!
Someone found a tiny otter.
Was she hit by a car?

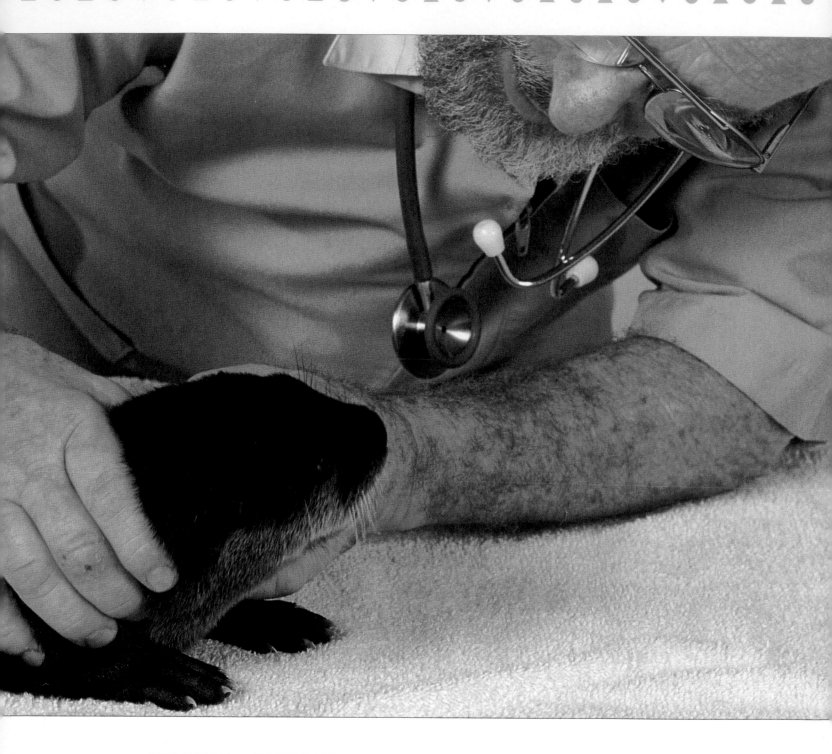

**CHEEE!  CHEEE!**

She's cold, hungry, and scared.

But she is not hurt.

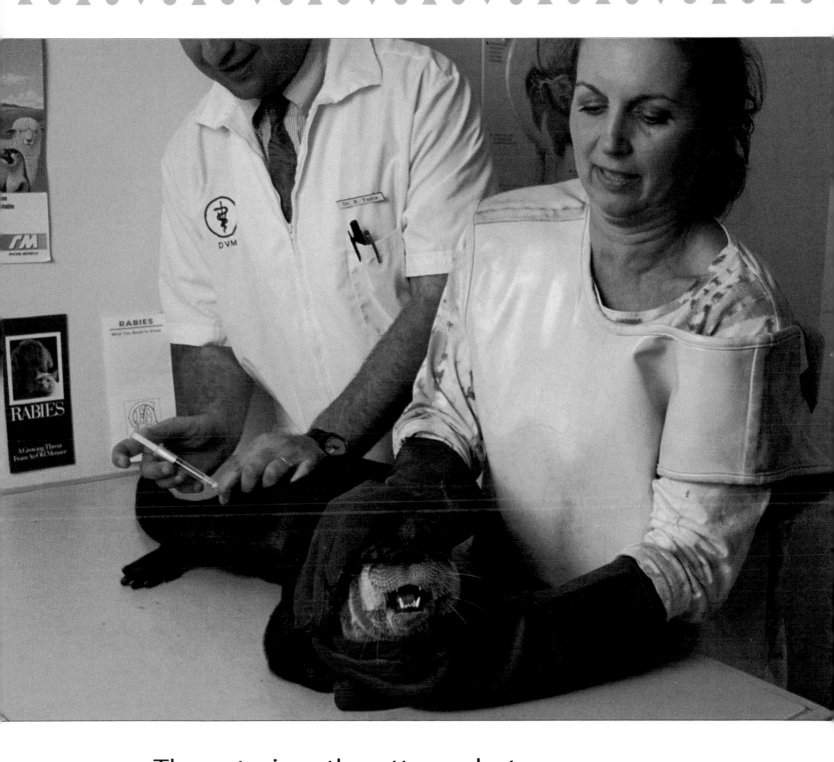

The vet gives the otter a shot.
A helper holds
the otter's head.

The tiny otter is warm and safe.
The vet is happy.

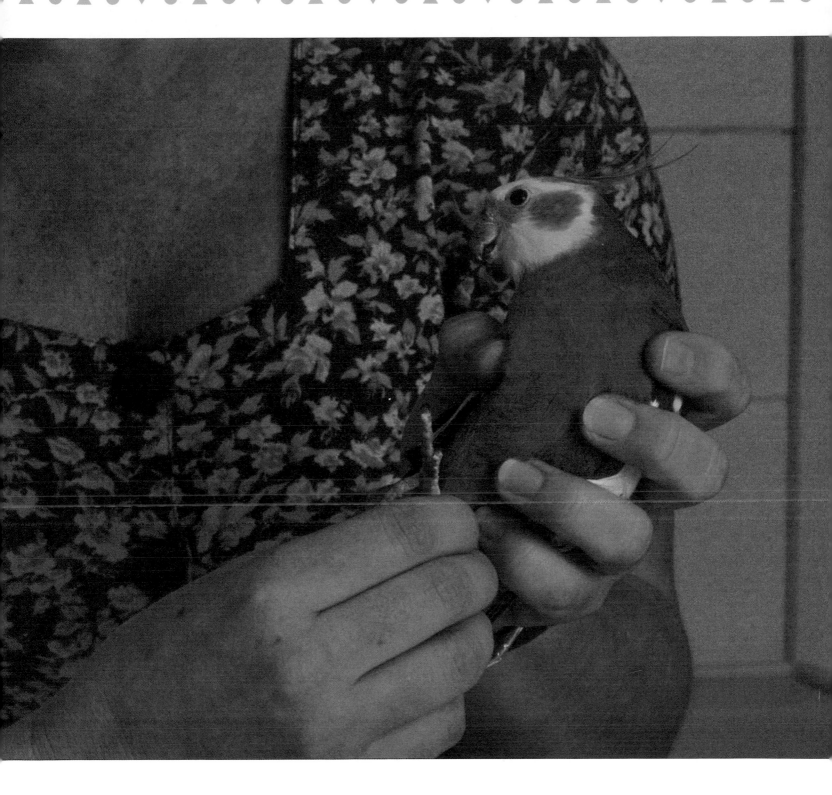

**SQUAWK!**

Gwennie has a sore foot.

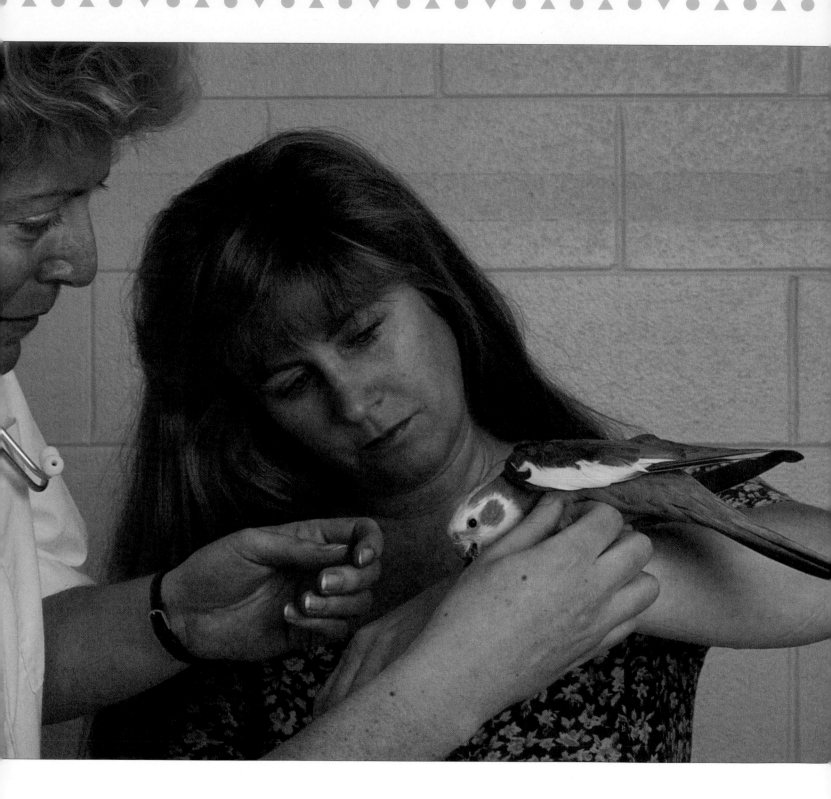

"Put this medicine on her foot for ten days,"
the vet tells Gwennie's owner.

What's in the pillowcase?

It's Joe, the opposum.   He has a sore foot too.

21

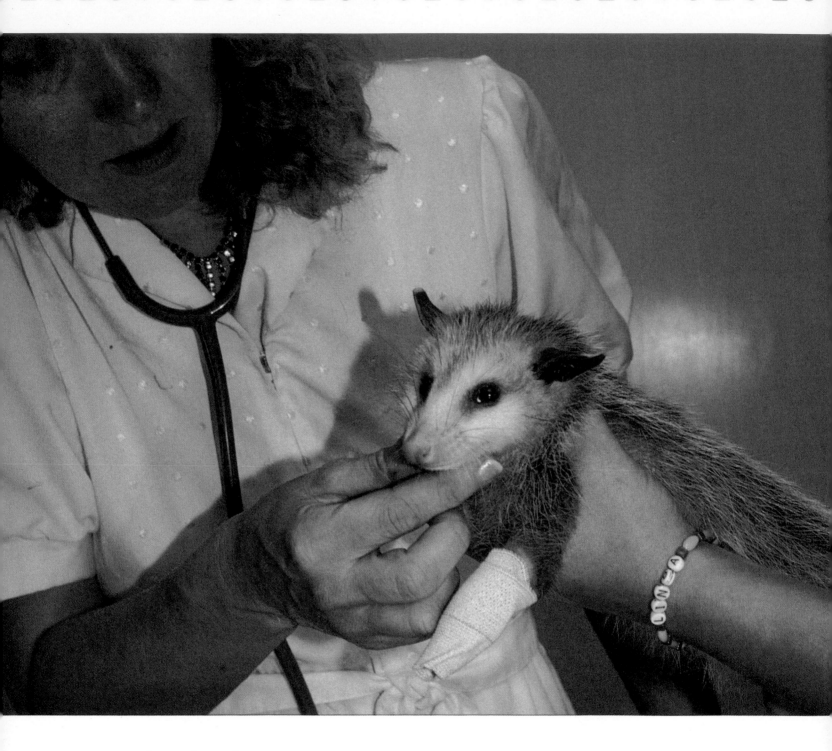

Joe is okay now.
Vets learn to work with many
kinds of animals.

This vet is worried about
Pat the cat.  He calls a friend who teaches
at a veterinary school.

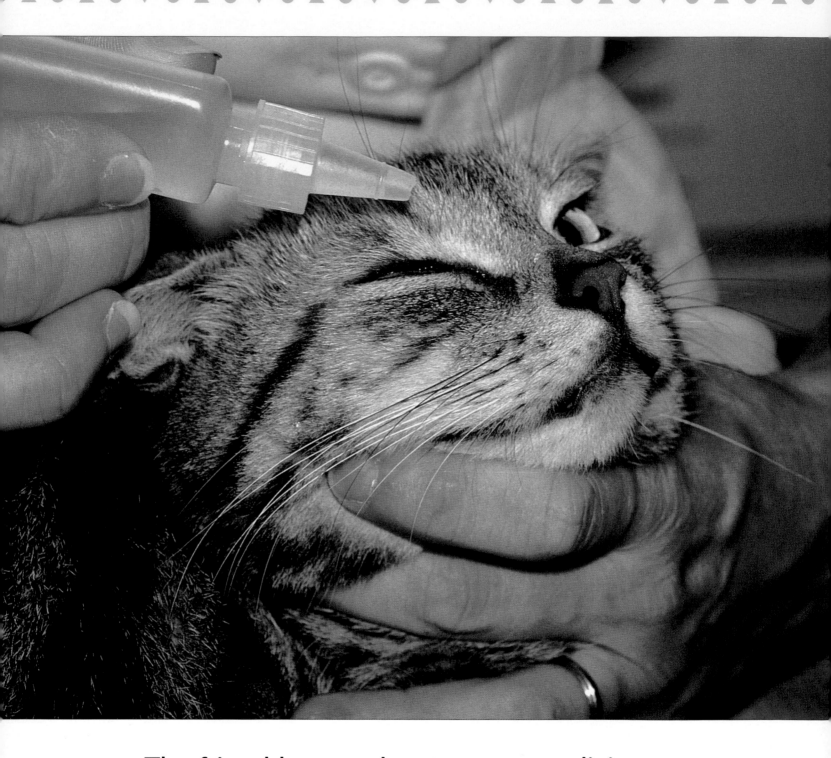

The friend knows about a new medicine.
"Good!" says the vet. "I'll try it on Pat."
Vets often help each other.

Evening comes.

This dog can go home.

He will be very happy to see his owner.

**ARF! ARF!**

"Andy's doing fine," says the vet.
"But give him this medicine with his food."

This tiny kitten is wide awake.
**MEOW! MEOW!**
she says.

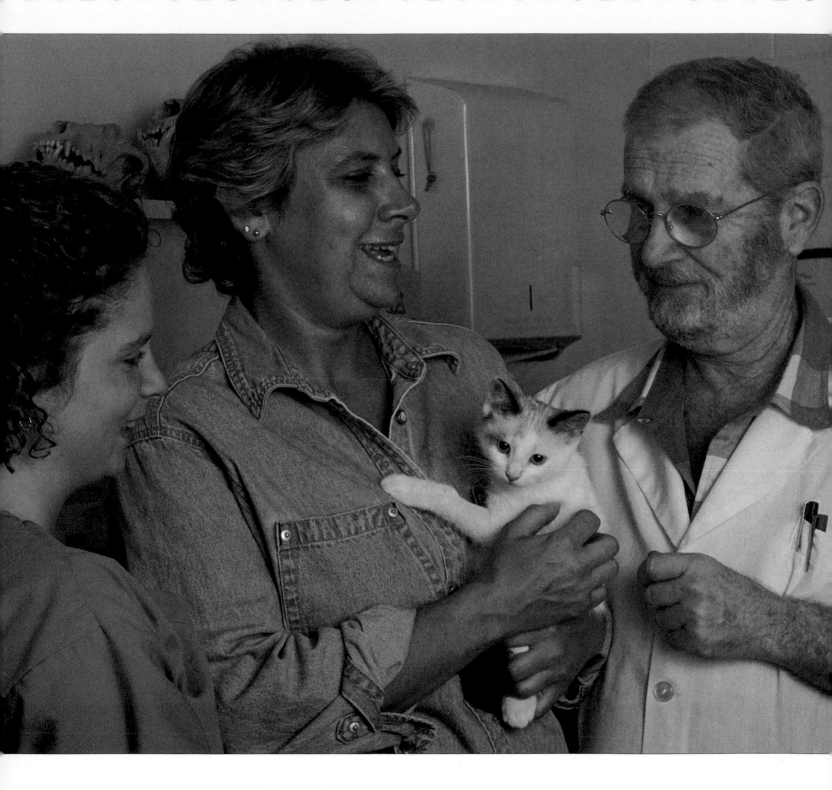

Everyone laughs.

The kitten is going to be fine too.

**WOOF!   ARF!   SQUAWK!   MEEE-OOOWWW!**
It is time for this vet to go home.

His own pets are waiting for him.

Veterinarians do love animals.

That's why they're vets!

## Questions and Answers

### What do veterinarians do?

Veterinarians treat sick and hurt animals. They also help keep healthy animals healthy. Some treat cats, dogs, and other pets. Other vets work with farm, zoo, or wild animals. Some teach in a veterinary school. Others do research.

### How do people learn to be veterinarians?

Most veterinarians go to college for two to four years. Then they go to veterinary school for four years. Vets must learn how animal's bodies are put together and how they work. They learn about animal diseases and what medicines they can use to make sick animals well. They learn how to set broken bones and how to do surgery. Finally, they must pass a test in the state where they will work.

### What kind of people are veterinarians?

Veterinarians are smart. They know about many kinds of animals. Vets are gentle, and good with their hands too. They might have to operate on a tiny bird. Veterinarians who work with large animals like cows and horses must be strong. Most of all, vets love animals and help them.

### How much money do veterinarians make?

Veterinarians just out of school make about $20,000 a year. Later they can make more than that. Some vets do their work for free. They volunteer. They treat homeless or wild animals.

## Glossary

**animal hospital**—a place that is built to help sick and hurt animals

**checkup**—a physical examination given by a doctor

**dentist**—a doctor who cleans and fixes teeth and gums

**healthy**—having no sickness caused by disease or pain caused by injury to the body

**medicine**—any pill, liquid, or salve used to heal a sickness or an injury

**operation**—a way of cutting into a body to fix something

**pill**—a small, solid object that holds medicine

**shot**—liquid medicine put into the body with a needle

**toothache**—pain in a tooth caused by a bad tooth or infected gums

**veterinary school**—a place where young students go in order to learn how to help sick and injured animals of all kinds

**CAROL GREENE** has written over 200 books for children. She also likes to read books, make teddy bears, work in her garden, and sing. Ms. Greene lives in Webster Groves, Missouri.